Wild River Bears

Inspirations of a Cancer Survivor

Changes

I am a cancer survivor who was given a second lease on life. My diagnosis came in December of 2008, and I am now in my seventh year of remission. I wrote this book to promote an optimistic view for others diagnosed with similar diseases, to encourage them in their recovery, and return to a productive lifestyle as soon as they can.

Cancer generally causes a change of one's philosophy of life. Once diagnosed, a person usually starts to think more earnestly about what will come after death. The diagnosis gives a feeling that no words can describe. In a way, cancer is an indefinable entity that appears from out of nowhere, pierces you firmly in its talons, and lifts you into the darkness of some unknown territory.

The immortal, forever young, and indestructible nature of our youth gives way to thoughts of hope for a new life after this physical existence passes away. As higher psychological distress and anxieties fill one's thoughts, existential questions become common in one's mind speak: things will now be weighed!

A diagnosis like cancer will cause most to experience substantial mental changes in life. All that matters is the truth. Now, the life you have lived more clearly defines your soul, so you make changes. Old philosophies are broken on this new reality as the mortal coil unwinds itself and becomes a thin, fragile thread. I have seen this in waiting rooms, infusion rooms, and at home on a death bed. I have found that simply being optimistic is the most beneficial mental state for decreasing psychological distress, as well as experiencing a better quality of life during recovery. As you enhance your quality of life by reducing isolation, managing stress with outlook, and at the same time developing new hopes, you will positively affect your immune system, gaining strength in the fight for recovery. Remember, cancer is afraid of a strong person, so show it your fighting spirit and unyielding will to live.

While receiving infusion and during some of the isolations after my treatment, I often thought about my family. My family was fractured, and when I was diagnosed, I was in a far-off place. After a few weeks of tests and biopsies I met with a my oncologist who assured me that my cancer was curable. I did not know that until then, and I still didn't quite buy it for a while; however, I was one of the lucky ones. Even so, I had a very harsh regimen of chemotherapy ahead of me.

And as I said, my thoughts were on my family. I was in Virginia, they were in Utah, and I wanted to get home. I booked a flight and left behind a perfectly good (actually fantastic) oncology center for the unknown. I got lucky again and was quickly picked up by a master of oncology in another great center that was close to home and family.

Cancer has its gifts. My gift was a reunion with my children, bringing us closer now than ever before. And back in Utah, I was free to focus my thoughts on my future. Before I had cancer, I was building skylights as a specialty contractor; but unable to go back to that occupation, I dwelled upon what was next for me. I concluded that I loved nature photography. I was good at it, and even though the field was saturated with photographers of every skill level, I convinced myself to move forward with a camera in hand, all the while thanking and praising God for his marvelous gifts and perfect creation.

I had always wanted to see and photograph spirit bears in their native habitat, so my post-cancer photography journey began at the Great Bear Rainforest with these beautiful creatures. Without much planning on my part the rest of my sojourn unfolded, and I feel I have been guided by God's Spirit through each phase.

"Though we travel the world over to find the beautiful, we must carry it with us, or we find it not."

—Ralph Waldo Emerson

CHAPTER 1

Road Trip

In early October 2011, I flew to Valdez, Alaska, to help my brother with his move back to Utah after he retired from the oil fields. I had been in remission from cancer for about a year and a half and I was beginning to feel stronger—at least strong enough for this trip. Having driven the Alcan Highway once before in 1980, and always wanting to make the trip once more, my brother and I planned the road trip. Any opportunities I have to spend time in Valdez, Alaska, with a camera in hand are days of my life well spent.

After arriving in Valdez I photographed black bears, eagles, sea lions, harbor seals, sea otters, and other creatures that are abundant in this region of the Prince William Sound. In the past I have spotted coastal brown bears, but from distances either too far for photography or at night. My prayers were answered this trip though, as a very photographable two-year-old cub made himself available near the fish hatchery on the Day Hill Road. After feeling relatively sure that this cub's mother had

abandoned him and he was therefore alone, I considered how to photograph him.

I was getting shots of sea otters on one side of the road when the small bear showed up to fish the river directly across the highway. The cub was large for his age and displayed a new fishing technique I had never witnessed before. He stretched himself horizontally across the rocks close to the river's edge. He seemed almost as capable at gripping the rocks with his hind feet as he was with his front feet; he really could hold on to the rocks! Until then I thought bear's hind feet were comparable to human feet, but as I discovered here they appeared to be much more dexterous; perhaps the difference was mostly in the claws. I couldn't say if his fishing technique worked for him because the only salmon he caught came after he crossed the river, at which time I was well on my way to the safety of the truck.

Only one road leads out of Valdez, Alaska: the Richardson Highway, going up the Lowe River basin through Keystone Canyon to a summit called Thompson Pass. Thompson Pass is amazing and beautiful as the mountains are freshly cut from the receding glacial ice age. These are rugged sharp peaks, jagged and steep and yet typical for the Chugach Range. Positioned along the Gulf of Alaska, the Chugach Mountains receive more snowfall than anywhere else in the world—an annual average of over 600 inches. The World Extreme Skiing Championship was held annually here. However, the area was deemed too remote and extreme to continue hosting this event so organizers moved it elsewhere.

The winter trek through Keystone Canyon is a dangerous venture—the threat of avalanche looming in winter and sudden rockslides in summer. Several times motorists have been trapped between two separate avalanches, living in mortal fear of more snow coming down on top of them. The beauties of these places have their extremes and nature often turns this beauty into the bait for fatal dangers.

While living in Valdez during the early 1980's I rescued many friends whose vehicles slid off the road in this canyon, coming danger-ously close to the canyon road's steep edge. I readily volunteered to tow them out during blizzards and whiteouts, knowing the longer their vehicles remained stuck in this canyon the greater the chance of an avalanche sweeping their vehicles over the edge to be crushed on the rocks deep in the canyon below. And now while traveling through this canyon again I had flashbacks to many past events, recalling how mentally and physically tough I once was. I got a real feel, which was also kind of chilling, as to just how much cancer has changed me.

During a previous trip to Valdez in 2008 I photographed the Worthington Glacier as my brother, his wife and I were driving to Anchorage where I was flying out to the East Coast for a medical evaluation related to injuries I received from an auto accident. Fresh snow had fallen overnight, but as we crossed over the pass rays of sunlight began to break through. This developed into the most

A curious sea otter raises itself high out of the water to investigate his surroundings near the fish hatchery at Valdez, Alaska. Sea otters can still be found in abundance in these waters.

*"Many men go fishing all of their lives
without knowing that it is not fish they are after."*
— Henry David Thoreau

*"Let yourself be silently drawn
by the stronger pull of what you really love."*
— Rumi

incredibly beautiful winter scene I had ever witnessed, and I captured the moment forever with my camera. The summits in the photos are headwaters, the glaciers and snowpacks that blanket the earth's mountains. Many streams, rivers, lakes, and alluvial underground aquifers begin at the Chugach Range, and the melt from the peaks surrounding Valdez is the best-tasting drinking water I have ever had. Upon every return trip I take a quiet moment just to make a toast to God with an ice-cold glass full of this perfectly blended mountain brew. Nothing tastes purer or more delicious to me than the simple tap water coming from the Mineral Creek drainage just outside Valdez.

In the course of this road trip from Valdez to my brother's new home in Utah, we encountered nature's abundant beauty at nearly every turn. Not driving at the time, I sat as a front-seat passenger taking it all in. We encountered owls, hawks, and eagles. Several small herds of barren ground caribou ran alongside the truck and a large bull with an impressive antler rack crossed right in front of the truck at dusk near the Tok Junction. We encountered rutting elk close to Whitehorse in the Yukon Territory. We saw and photographed numerous wood bison, stone sheep, and mountain caribou near Stone Mountain Provincial Park. We came across a very large and beautiful reddish-blonde wolf feeding on road kill in northern Alberta. And now, recounting this rare encounter, I quietly laugh to myself, remembering how we muffed up the photo-op with this wolf (can't get them all). We also happened upon several red foxes and an abundant white-tailed deer population, stopping many times just to take in the scenery and snap a few photos. Time during this trip passed pleasantly.

"Everything is flowing—going somewhere, animals and so-called lifeless rocks as well as water. Thus the snow flows fast or slow in grand beauty-making glaciers and avalanches; the air in majestic floods carrying minerals, plant leaves, seeds, spores, with streams of music and fragrance; water streams carrying rocks...while the stars go streaming through space pulsed on and on forever like blood...in nature's warm heart."
—John Muir

The Worthington Glacier located at the summit of Thompson's Pass.

"Sunshine cannot bleach the snow, Nor time unmake what poets know."

— Ralph Waldo Emerson

This image was photographed from the same tripod setting moments before the Worthington Glacier image was taken. Thompson Pass is worth seeing any time of year.

"Love is life's snow. It falls deepest and softest into the gashes left by the fight —whiter and purer than snow itself."

— Fridtjof Nansen

Before this trip started I convinced my brother that we needed to make a slight detour through Jasper National Park in Alberta. We decided to spend two extra days there to appreciate the natural wonders of the Jasper/Banff area. And even two days was not enough time for a place like this—a place I consider to be the pinnacle of the Rockies.

Entering from the north we drove south through the park and came across a small band of bighorn sheep with two very large rams. These two monarchs were at the bank of the Athabasca River when we found them watering and casually browsing. I photographed them for an hour as they hiked back up to their beds on a nearby ridge. These experiences helped me forget all about the pain of infusion needles, the constant nausea, that awful chemo aftertaste—and all the stress, worry, exhaustion, and conversation of cancer.

Arriving in Jasper, we secured lodging and set out to find and photograph rutting elk. We found elk in abundance, but the rut was clearly over. We departed early the next morning for Maligne Lake, arriving just before dawn. This lake and the surrounding area are so beautiful that words are wasted trying to do them justice. It's a see-it-to-believe-it place of astonishing panoramic beauty, with the lake seeming to have one shoreline on Earth and the opposite in Heaven.

Last year during a trip to Jasper Park in the fall of 2012, I found a multicolored grizzly bear working the berry patches along the road at the summit by the Maligne Lake parking area. Farther down the road I found several black bears filling up on the abundant berries, fattening up their bodies for winter's long nap. During other trips in the past I found moose rutting not far down the road from the lake, and on this trip with my brother we came across a cow moose with her calf. In just two days of touring this provincial park my brother and I had seen coyotes, bighorns, mountain goats, white-tailed deer, mule deer, abundant elk, a black bear, moose, and scenery sliced right out of Heaven and placed on Earth.

This two-year-old cub easily crossed the fast moving creek. Obstacles like swift currents seem like an adequate protective barrier to humans when in fact they are no barrier at all to a bear.

On our final day in Jasper, after a stop at Athabasca Falls, we got back on the road to Utah. Nearing the summit close to the Columbia Icefield, we hit photographic pay dirt: a blonde mother grizzly and her two grown blonde cubs walking next to the road along the Athabasca River. And talk about icing on the cake—a fresh blanket of snow covered everything except the river, which was a beautiful glacier ice blue in color. I took hundreds of photos.

These bears seemed mostly unconcerned that we were there. They journeyed toward their den site with thick pelts and fat bodies. Of the hundreds of photos I snapped of the trio about 40 are real wall-hangers, stunningly sharp and well-composed. When the grizzlies reached the Athabasca Glacier they crossed the road and climbed the mountain toward Wilcox Pass and vanished.

The Columbia Icefield is a massive glacial aquifer located in the Canadian Rockies astride the Continental Divide of North America. The ice field lies partly in the northwestern tip of Banff National Park and the southern end of Jasper National Park. It is about 325 km² in area, 100 to 365 meters (328 to 1,197 ft.) in depth, and receives up to seven meters (275 in.) of snowfall per year. This ice field fodders eight major glaciers, including: the Columbia Icefield itself, the Athabasca Glacier, Castleguard Glacier, Columbia Glacier, Dome Glacier, Stutfield Glacier, and the Saskatchewan Glacier.

The Athabasca River and the North Saskatchewan River originate in the Columbia Icefield, as do the tributary headwaters of the Columbia River. As the ice field is atop a triple Continental Divide, these waters flow ultimately north to the Arctic Ocean, east to Hudson Bay (and thence to the North Atlantic Ocean), and south and west to the Pacific Ocean. Hudson Bay, in some watershed divisions, is considered to be in the Arctic watershed, which arguably makes this a triple Continental Divide point.

The rest of the road trip seemed uneventful as we drove the I-15 corridor through Montana, Idaho, and northern Utah. I reveled in writing about this road trip as it brought back to me many delightful memories.

Far left: A young stone sheep ram watches us from above the road in Stone Mountain Provincial Park, British Columbia, Canada. Stone Sheep (Ovis dalli stonei) are closely related to the whitish cream-colored Dall Sheep (Ovis dalli dalli) that are found farther to the north. These two sheep species make up what are called the "thin-horned" sheep, as opposed to those with massive horns like North America's bighorn sheep.

Center: Mountain Caribou depend upon large tracts of old-growth forest in what is termed the "Interior Wet Belt" of the northern Rockies of British Columbia. These interior humid forests have dwindled over the last century and Mountain Caribou numbers are respectively in decline. Mountain Caribou differ from their cousin species in that they do not migrate great distances, making them a key indicator species to the health of this region.

Right: This was the smaller of the two large Bighorn Sheep rams that greeted my brother and I as we entered Jasper Provincial Park. Fortunately, Bighorn Sheep are still found abundantly in their home ranges as a result of cooperative conservation efforts.

Pre-dawn at Maligne Lake, October, 2011. Being there always feels like standing at heaven's gate.

"Heaven-born, the soul a heavenward course must hold; beyond the world she soars; the wise man, I affirm, can find no rest in that which perishes, nor will he lend his heart to ought that doth time depend."

— Michelangelo

Pre-dawn at Maligne Lake, September, 2012.
"How glorious a greeting the sun gives the mountains!"
— John Muir

Grizzly sow with both of her second year cubs crossing the headwaters of the Athabasca River in the Athabasca Glacier moraine ice field.

"Pursue some path, however narrow and crooked,
in which you can walk with love and reverence."

— Henry David Thoreau

Every time I see wild bears in native habitat I feel enriched. I believe these experiences will remain embedded in my soul for eternity.

"Forests, lakes, and rivers, clouds and winds, stars and flowers, stupendous glaciers and crystal snowflakes—every form of animate or inanimate existence, leaves its impress upon the soul of man."

— Orison Swett Marden

"I wanted to be the first to view a country on which the eyes of a white man had never gazed and to follow the course of rivers that run through a new land."

— Jedediah Smith

"And the point is to live everything. Live the questions now. Perhaps then, someday far into the future, you will gradually, without even noticing it, live your way into the answer."

— Rainer Maria Rilke, *Letters to a Young Poet*

"The first and fundamental law of Nature,
which is, to seek peace and follow it."
— Thomas Hobbes

"I've spent most of my life surrounded by incredible beauty, enjoying wonderful relationships with wild animals most of us were taught to fear. We really need to get over our fear of the wild. It's what sustains us; not what threatens us."

— Charlie Russell

CHAPTER 2

Inspirations, Thoughts and Images

"Life can only be understood backwards; but it must be lived forwards."
— Søren Kierkegaard

"There are only two ways to live your life. One is as though nothing is a miracle. The other is as though everything is a miracle."

— Albert Einstein

"I think that I cannot preserve my health and spirits, unless I spend four hours a day at least—and it is commonly more than that—sauntering through the woods and over the hills and fields, absolutely free from all worldly engagements."

— *Henry David Thoreau*

"The people that walked in darkness have seen a great light:
they that dwell in the land of the shadow of death,
upon them hath the light shined."

— Isaiah 9: 2

"There are two types of fisherman—those who fish for sport and those who fish for fish.
— Author Unknown

"Now I see the secret of making the best person,
it is to grow in the open air and to eat and sleep with the earth."
— Walt Whitman

Right: I had hoped to photograph one bear in my life that qualified as a true giant; one over ten foot. On my recent trip to Katmai National Park I photographed two, and this beautiful blond boar pictured here fishing in the Brooks River, was the smaller of the two. This bear, the rangers assured me, is a ten-and-a-half foot beast. Earlier the same day we encountered a bruin the Rangers said to be well over 11 foot.

"Believe one who knows; you will find something greater in woods than in books.
Trees and stones will teach you that which you can never learn from masters."

— St. Bernard de Clairvaux

"Live in the sunshine, swim the sea, drink the wild air."
— Ralph Waldo Emerson

"We don't receive wisdom; we must discover it for ourselves after a journey that no one can take for us or spare us."

— Marcel Proust

" The charm of fishing is that it is the pursuit of what is elusive but attainable, a perpetual series of occasions for hope."

— John Buchan

An explosion of water, fish, and bear as this young grizzly submerged herself completely, then abruptly broke the surface lock jawed on a struggling fish.

"Life in us is like the water in a river."
— Henry David Thoreau

"These woods are lovely, dark and deep,
But I have promises to keep,
And miles to go before I sleep,
And miles to go before I sleep."
— Robert Frost

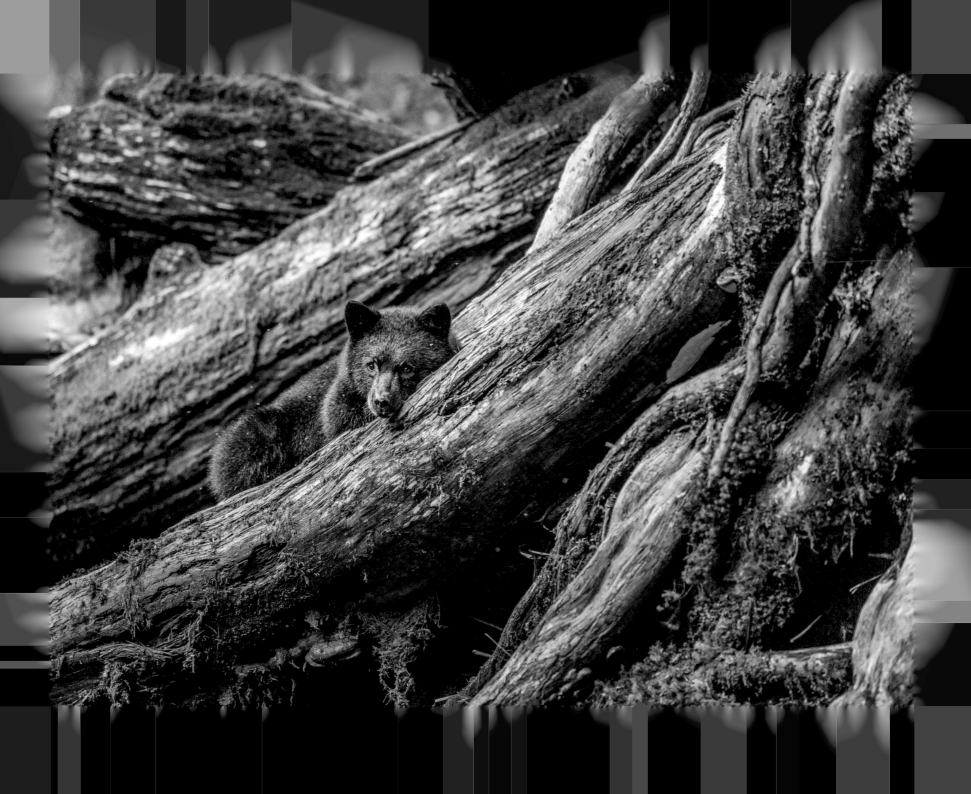

"I THINK that I shall never see
A poem lovely as a tree.
A tree whose hungry mouth is prest
Against the sweet earth's flowing breast;

A tree that looks at God all day,
And lifts her leafy arms to pray;
A tree that may in summer wear
A nest of robins in her hair;

Upon whose bosom snow has lain;
Who intimately lives with rain.
Poems are made by fools like me,
But only God can make a tree."

— Joyce Kilmer

"Hope is the thing with feathers,
That perches in the soul,
And sings the tune without the words,
And never stops at all."

— Emily Dickinson

"The madness of the eyes is the lure of the abyss. Sirens lurk in the dark depths of the pupils as they lurk at the bottom of the sea, that I know for sure - but I have never encountered them, and I am searching still for the profound and plaintive gazes in whose depths I might be able, like Hamlet redeemed, to drown the Ophelia of my desire."

— Jean Lorrain, Monsieur De Phocas

"There is a pleasure in the pathless woods,
There is a rapture on the lonely shore,
There is society where none intrudes,
By the deep sea, and music in its roar:
I love not man the less, but Nature more."
 — Lord Byron

CHAPTER 3

Riparian Woodlands

A TREE IS A CORPOREAL FACTORY living its life in three different zones. First, trees receive solar energy from the sky above them to produce, through a process of photosynthesis, stored energy in the form of chlorophyll. Secondly, trees absorb water, minerals, and nutrients through their root systems below the ground's surface, an area called the lithosphere. Lastly, trees gather carbon dioxide, some through their roots, but mostly from the air around them, breathing in carbon dioxide and releasing oxygen through their leaves in a process called respiration. Trees then convert the carbon dioxide into organic compounds—sugars—in a process called carbon fixation. The ingredients gathered from these three zones are then blended to make seeds, leaves, needles, bark, sap, nuts, fruits, flowers, nectar, pollen, and wood fibers. This factory blending process is called biosynthesis, a process which catalyzes enzymes, turning substrates into more complex products within a living organism.

Each individual tree has a water cycle of its own and is a part of its respective regional water cycle, and also part of the global water cycle. Trees have a daily cycle, a seasonal cycle, and an annual cycle for storing groundwater and releasing that water by evaporating the groundwater back into the atmosphere. A large, leafy tree may take up as much as one ton of water from the soil every day. A typical tree breathes out 250 to 400 or more gallons of water per day. You may not see a tree performing as a faucet, but in many regards that is one of their key functions.

Trees are also the first defense against soil erosion, especially along riverbanks. They are like an army in the service of the earth, but even so, deserts are spreading at the rate of five million hectares a year worldwide (not yet quite as fast as the forests are vanishing). The trouble with reforestation is that it is a biologically simple replacement for a richly diverse, mature forest; micro-ecosystems that have taken centuries to establish vanish into the thin air of what some are calling progress. Where large areas of trees are removed, rain will become less frequent or completely cease downwind. Therefore, the helter-skelter method of forest management is clearly not the best way to approach forest product conservation.

Trees humidifying the air miles inland maintain the rain cycle far from oceans in a process called evapotranspiration. Even near oceans, trees play a vital role in producing rain and re-humidifying the air. Along with the influence of oceans, trees play the other critical part in the water cycle across the earth.

A wild river system would not be complete without an accompanying old-growth forest somewhere along its path. The two are symbiotically interconnected and together form the rich environments called riparian woodlands. Riparian is defined as a riverbank ecosystem that contains water-dependent, woody plants. Riparian zones are important sources and storage sites for the nutrients and energy necessary for organic life.

Along riverbanks, trees help to change the chemical balance of the water; they extract minerals and organic nutrients from the soil and deposit them into rivers and streams. Trees on the river's edge also have a far-reaching, positive effect on the biological health of the river. Predators such as salmonid fish feed on invertebrates that fall into the water from the branches and leaves of trees overhead. Along with other life forms, these kinds of fish gain shade and shelter from the undercuts and pools created from riverbank trees. Shade is important in at least two ways—it regulates water temperature and balances the growth of water weeds. Overheating of the water is prevented by overhanging canopies; these leafy coverings also discourage the loss of dissolved oxygen in the water. Leaf litter from nearby trees is foundational to a river's food chain. Quite often, upland streams are too cold or nutrient poor to facilitate plant growth, so leaf litter becomes a primary energy source.

In the water, microorganisms and invertebrates decompose leaf litter. Bacteria and filamentous fungi work first to condition the leaves. Next, invertebrates classified as shredders and collectors are able to break down the leaf litter. These organisms include the larvae forms of mayflies, mosquitoes, water beetles, dragonflies, caddis flies, stoneflies, chironomids, and midges.

A diversity of trees along a river is advantageous because different leaves decay at different rates. This variance in timing provides a food source in streams during the winter. Dead wood, which falls into a stream, creates a more valuable biological environment. The flow of water in a stream can be slowed by woody debris, forming still pools, which some fish utilize for spawning. Additional benefits of dead wood include shelter from predatory birds and mammals; a greater number of territories for fish, as more fish will occupy an area if they cannot see one another; and the ability to trap organic matter, increasing the amount of food at the bottom of the food chain. Riparian forests reduce sedimentation in streambeds, thus protecting spawning beds for native and the ocean-going species of fish.

In most natural streams and rivers dead wood is an abundant substrate with key benefits for the instream environment. Dead wood has substantial impact upon channel forming processes and the formation of the river's flow structure. Dead wood also provides refuge, habitat diversity, and food for aquatic organisms. Its presence enhances all aquatic biodiversity.

Rutting elk cool off in the Athabasca River just outside of Jasper, Alberta.

"Color is my daylong obsession, joy, and torment."
— Claude Monet

A bull moose drinks fresh snow melted waters that seep into Silver Lake from the surrounding mountains. I call the structure that I'm standing on to take this image "Deidre's Bridge" after my granddaughter. Together we have watched many moose from it.

"I like this place and could willingly waste my time in it."
— William Shakespeare

This is the largest wild bear that I have witnessed to date. Unfortunately, my photos fall short of fully representing his immense size. I was on a platform overlooking the Brooks River at Katmai National Park, Alaska with five large bears fishing the river in front of me when this behemoth emerged from the woods. All five bears stopped what they were doing and one by one peeled off to fish elsewhere. The big boar waited for the subordinates to depart and then calmly entered the river and fished solitaire. The ranger who was with us on the platform said that this bear's size has been estimated to be over eleven feet squared, which is actually a square of the hide size: the length from tip of nose to tip of tail, plus the length from the tips of both front paws stretched out, and that sum divided by two. A live bear's size is an estimate calculated from the bear's tracks.

Life is all about fresh drinking water, with only three percent of the Earth's water qualifying as fresh water, and slightly over two thirds of this is frozen in glaciers and polar ice caps. The remaining fresh water is found mainly as groundwater, with only a small fraction present above ground or in the atmosphere.

*"Enjoy thy stream, O harmless fish;
And when an angler for his dish,
Through gluttony's vile sin,
Attempts, the wretch, to pull thee out,
God give thee strength, O gentle trout,
To pull the rascal in!"*
— John Wolcot

"For a century, environmentalism has divided itself into warring camps: conservationists versus preservationists.... The struggle pits those who would meddle with nature against those who would leave it be.... The only sensible way forward lies in a melding of the two philosophies. If nature has grown artificial, then restoring wilderness requires human intervention. We must manage nature in order to leave it alone."

— David Baron

"But mighty Nature bounds as from her birth;
The sun is in the heavens, and life on earth:
Flowers in the valley, splendor in the beam,
Health on the gale, and freshness in the stream."
— Lord Byron

"It is the mark of an educated mind to be able to entertain a thought without accepting it."
— Aristotle

"We did not think of the great open plains, the beautiful rolling hills, and winding streams with tangled growth, as "wild." Only to the white man was nature a "wilderness" and only to him was the land "infested" with "wild" animals and "savage" people. To us it was tame. Earth was bountiful and we were surrounded with the blessings of the Great Mystery. Not until the hairy man from the east came and with brutal frenzy heaped injustices upon us and the families we loved was it "wild" for us. When the very animals of the forest began fleeing from his approach, then it was that for us the "Wild West" began."

— Chief Luther Standing Bear – Oglala Sioux

"But the old Lakota was wise. He knew that the man's heart, away from nature, becomes hard, he knew that lack of respect from growing, living things soon led to a lack of respect for humans, too. So he kept his children close to nature's softening influence."

— Chief Luther Standing Bear – Oglala Sioux

"I do not exist to impress the world.
I exist to live my life in a way that will make me happy."

— Richard Bach

"How beautifully leaves grow old.
How full of light and color are their last days."

— John Burroughs

On Princess Royal Island, the Spirit Bears have never been hunted. These bears have a very passive nature toward humans.

CHAPTER 4

Spirit Bear Rainforest

THE SPIRIT BEARS, also called Kermode bears, are found in the Great Bear Rainforest of coastal British Columbia. Spirit bears are not albino but a cream-colored variant of black bears, and they are rarer than pandas. Only one in ten black bears on the Princess Royal Island are born as a spirit bear. On other islands and areas of the Great Bear Rainforest, the ratio of black to white bears varies. During my four-day tour, it was my utmost privilege to see even one, let alone photograph three different individuals. And although I did not see a cub spirit bear, and was thus unable to photograph a mother-cub mixture of black and white, I do have an image of what I believe are two grown siblings fishing close together. That particular snapshot appears within this chapter. I had hoped to capture these two fishing from the same rock, but the bears did not make eye contact with each other, and as the black color phase moved closer to the spirit bear, the latter turned and moved downstream.

The ecosystem of the Great Bear Rainforest is shaped primarily by the Pacific Ocean. Next to plankton, salmon are the most important keystone species of this region, as they are a primary food source for hundreds of other species. Salmon carry vital nutrients from the ocean inland, up the numerous rivers and streams where they spawn. Bears grow fat on spawning salmon and eagles congregate en masse to harvest this deep ocean gift.

While photographing the Princess Royal Island, I witnessed Steller's Jays, Dippers, and Dolly Varden Trout all harvesting salmon eggs fresh from the stream. The jays carried away mouthfuls to hide for their winter food storage. And having seen very few pine martens in the wild, I was delighted to witness so many in one place, feeding on the salmon remains left behind by the bears, the chewy tails seeming to be their treat of choice.

I was impressed with this coastal forest ecosystem because to me the biodiversity felt complete and in harmony with the Creator's intended purpose. Even those nasty, biting black flies and mosquitoes that seem to have been designed in hell fill a vital role there, as all things are connected. Besides being key pollinators, the flies lay eggs in the salmon carcasses left behind by feeding wildlife. The eggs hatch into small larva, which in turn become a vital food source for the newly hatched and developing salmon fry. Everything connects in the riparian forest; everything is important, and everything there is vitally important to all of us, no matter where we live on this planet.

"The question is not what you look at, but what you see."
— Henry David Thoreau

I was born upon thy bank, river,
My blood flows in thy stream,
And thou meanderest forever,
At the bottom of my dream.

— Henry David Thoreau, *Journals 1906*, 1842 entry

"The mystical trend of our time, which shows itself particularly in the rampant growth of the so-called Theosophy and Spiritualism, is for me no more than a symptom of weakness and confusion. Since our inner experiences consist of reproductions, and combinations of sensory impressions, the concept of a soul without a body seems to me to be empty and devoid of meaning."

— Albert Einstein, letter of February 5, 1921

*"I'd rather be on the water thinkin' about God
than in church thinkin' about fishing."*
— Unknown

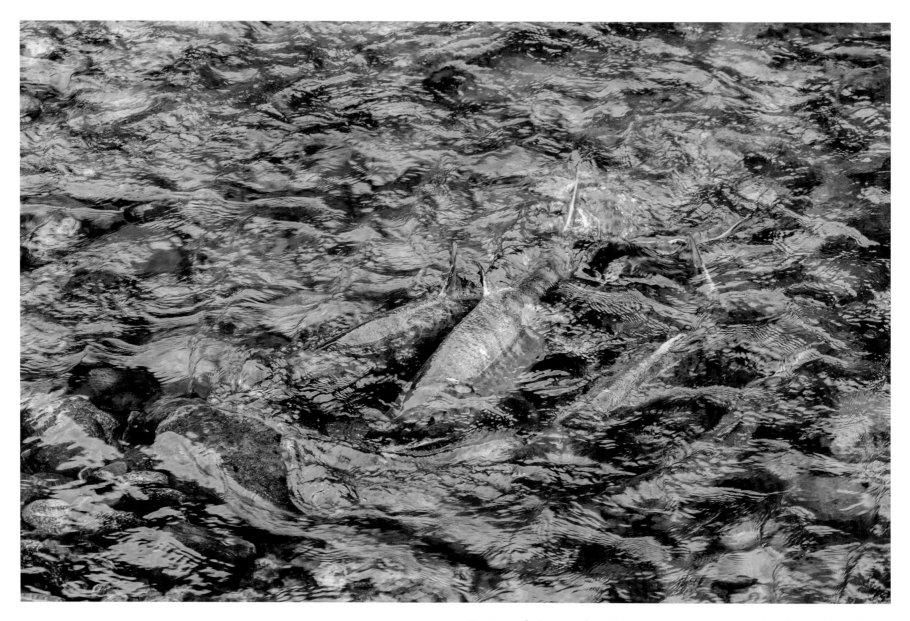

Five types of salmon are found off the western coast of North America: Sockeye Salmon (Oncorhynchus nerka) commonly called Red Salmon; Pink Salmon (O. gorbuscha) commonly called Pink or Humpback Salmon; Chum Salmon (O. ketal) commonly called Dog Salmon; Coho Salmon (O. kisutch) commonly called Silver Samon; and Chinook Salmon (O. tshawytscha) commonly called King Salmon.

"Write it on your heart that every day is the best day in the year.
He is rich who owns the day."

— Ralph Waldo Emerson

"Wonderful how completely everything in wild nature fits into us, as if truly part and parent of us. The sun shines not on us but in us. The rivers flow not past, but through us, thrilling, tingling, vibrating every fiber and cell of the substance of our bodies, making them glide and sing. The trees wave and the flowers bloom in our bodies as well as our souls, and every bird song, wind song, and; tremendous storm song of the rocks in the heart of the mountains is our song, our very own, and sings our love."

— John Muir, *Mountain Thoughts*

"This grand show is eternal. It is always sunrise somewhere; the dew is never dried all at once; a shower is forever falling; vapor is ever rising. Eternal sunrise, eternal dawn and gloaming, on sea and continents and islands, each in its turn, as the round earth rolls."

— John Muir

Salmon tails seemed to be the hors d'oeuvres at the Spirit Bear Rain forest.

"They are only resolute they shall eat
That they and their mates may thrive,
And they know that the dead are safer meat
Than the weakest thing alive."

— Rudyard Kipling

This eagle and crow provide us with a glimpse of the nutritional pecking order present in most northern coastal rivers.

"In the midst of chaos, there is also opportunity."
— Sun Tzu

CHAPTER 5

Wild Rivers

A WILD RIVER is a river or a river system designated by a government to be protected and kept relatively untouched by development, and is, therefore, in near natural condition, with all or most of its natural values intact. The term "wild river" may also more generically describe rivers which provide a wilderness type experience or have a wilderness type quality which may be considered worth protecting and keeping for future generations. A wild river flows freely without dams.

Two of the rivers featured in this book are also natural spawning habitats for native salmon populations. So I would add to the definition that a wild river maintains its historic status as spawning grounds for all native species of fish. In northwest America, salmon are a keystone species, which means the impact they have on other life is greater than would be expected in relation to their biomass. The death of salmon is consequential. Salmon carcasses are rich in nutrients like nitrogen, sulfur, carbon, and phosphorus; these vital elements are transferred from the ocean to wildlife such as bears, eagles, and all creatures living close to the riparian woodlands and all areas found adjacent to the rivers. This has secondary or incidental effects not only for the next generation of salmon, but for every species living in the riparian zones.

I know I am truly having a wilderness experience when I see bears fishing a river in the same manner as generations of their ancestors. The rivers on this blue planet of ours are more than just arteries of essential lifeblood flowing through the land masses; they are engines of biodiversity affecting all the earth's life and ecosystems in ways we do not fully understand.

"My religion consists of a humble admiration of the illimitable superior spirit who reveals himself in the slight details we are able to perceive with our frail and feeble minds."

— Albert Einstein

"Bears are not companions of men, but children of God, and His charity is broad enough for both.... We seek to establish a narrow line between ourselves and the feathery zeros we dare to call angels, but ask a partition barrier of infinite width to show the rest of creation its proper place. Yet bears are made of the same dust as we, and breathe the same winds and drink of the same waters. A bears days are warmed by the same sun, his dwellings are overdomed by the same blue sky, and his life turns and ebbs with heart-pulsings like ours and was poured from the same fountain...."

— John Muir

This little bear was named Casper; the tour guides felt that this young grizzly was light colored enough that she qualified as a Spirit Bear, and I agree.

"To be yourself in a world that is constantly trying to make you something else is the greatest accomplishment."

— Ralph Waldo Emerson

"Everything in . . . nature, is descended out that which is eternal, and stands as a . . . visible outbirth of it, so when we know how to separate out the grossness, death, and darkness . . . from it, we find . . . it in its eternal state."

— William Law

"The woods were made for the hunters of dreams,
The brooks for the fishers of song;
To the hunters who hunt for the gunless game
The streams and the woods belong."

— Sam Walter Foss

This is Casper in her second season of life.

"I think she is growing up, and so begins to dream dreams, and have hopes and fears and fidgets, without knowing why or being able to explain them."

— Louisa May Alcott

"We need the tonic of wildness.... At the same time that we are earnest to explore and learn all things, we require that all things be mysterious and unexplorable, that land and sea be indefinitely wild, unsurveyed and unfathomed by us because unfathomable. We can never have enough of nature."

— Henry David Thoreau, *Walden: Life in the Woods*

"I found in myself, and still find, an instinct toward a higher, or, as it is named, spiritual life, as do most men, and another toward a primitive rank and savage one, and I reverence them both. I love the wild not less than the good."

Henry David Thoreau, *Walden: Life in the Woods*

"It is not so much for its beauty that the forest makes a claim upon men's hearts, as for that subtle something, that quality of air that emanation from old trees, that so wonderfully changes and renews a weary spirit."

— Robert Louis Stevenson

"It's spring fever. That is what the name of it is. And when you've got it, you want—oh, you don't quite know what it is you do want, but it just fairly makes your heart ache, you want it so!"

— Mark Twain

Sometimes it seemed like a great door opened and a bear materialized, then just as fast as the bear appeared, it would step back into the shadows and trees, and the door would close.

"Time is but the stream I go a-fishing in. I drink at it; but while I drink I see the sandy bottom and detect how shallow it is. Its thin current slides away, but eternity remains."

— Henry David Thoreau, *Walden*

Bears navigate the world with their noses, including their water world.

"Memories, imagination, old sentiments, and associations are more readily reached through the sense of smell than through any other channel."
— Oliver Wendell Holmes

CHAPTER 6

Bear Olfaction and Taste

A BEAR'S SENSE OF SMELL is currently acknowledged as the best olfaction mechanism on Earth. I cannot say for sure if a grizzly bear's nose is any better than a black bear's nose, but I think grizzly bears have the edge. I once saw a large grizzly bear in the Lamar Valley of Yellowstone rear up and sniff the air for a brief second, then drop back on all fours and run for several miles to an elk carcass that was left mostly submerged in the Lamar River by the wolves that killed it. This is typical, and bears can smell food from even greater distances; some observers say that they have observed hungry bears smelling a fresh carcass from a distance of 20 miles. Polar bears might be the champs in the bear world for long-distance odor detection, but a polar bear's environment has far fewer competing and distracting odors than the mountains, forests, or coastal environments that other bears inhabit.

Olfaction and taste are both a form of chemoreception. The chemicals themselves that activate the olfactory system are called odorants— chemical vapors that are detected at very low concentrations. The part of a bear's brain that processes odorants is called the olfactory bulb. In bears, this mechanism is five times larger than its human equivalent. And with a human brain being over three times larger than a bear's brain these proportional olfactory bulb size differences become even more impressive.

Anatomy gives the grizzly bear a major advantage in olfaction by naturally equipping them with two nine-inch-long nostril channels to process odors. These extra-long nose channels have hundreds of times the surface area of a human's nose, allowing for more chemical odors to gather in bear noses. These odorants are then gathered to an area where ten million nerve strands and a billion receptor cells shoot electrical signals into the bear's brain. These signals travel along countless tiny pathways and end up on the brain's cribriform plate — the name given to a specific area of the skull responsible for separating the brain from the nasal cavity. Eventually, the information from the odors arrive at the gray matter of a bear's brain, which is a much larger gray matter than that found in most other animals. This gray matter allows bears to remember things like where to find food and shelter, or how to distinguish potential threats from other animals.

During a recent trip to British Columbia, I photographed a mother grizzly bear and her yearling cub using both their tongue and nostril in tandem while searching for salmon; three of these photographs appear in this chapter. Taste and smell are both chemical senses; they both give the brain information about the chemical composition of the surroundings. Smell is a more distant sense allowing creatures to detect small concentrations of airborne substances, whereas taste is an immediate sense usually used to check the acceptability of food before it enters the body. Taste and smell are only separated on land. Underwater, all chemicals are dissolved in the water, so there is no need for two separate sensory mechanisms and no reason for a land animal not to use both nose and tongue in tandem while submerged to gain enhanced reception of odor producing chemicals. Although hard to tell, I believe I saw several bears with their tongues extended while underwater as they searched for salmon. They may have been searching specifically for roe-bearing salmon or just using every advantage to detect and pinpoint a meal in the fast-moving current

of the river. Memories of tastes and smells are among the most persistent and indicative of all sensory memories, so a bear is more than adequately equipped to hunt for food underwater.

When humans and animals are afraid or stressed, we both give off air borne chemicals that most animals can detect. These are pheromones and can alert a bear and other creatures of the present threat level or potential for danger when close encounters with other creatures occur. When photographing bears, I often see them extend their tongues. This is to gather information as rapidly as they can to send to their Jacobson's organ which is a pheromone receptor located at the roof of their mouths. Animal pheromones are mainly emitted during estrus, but there are also alarm pheromones signaling stress or fear, food-trail pheromones, and pheromones that trigger societal response and other subtle communications within members of the same species.

The black pad on the bear's snout is equipped with hundreds of nimble muscles. These muscles are dexterous and allow a bear to manipulate its nostrils with the same nimble agility people use to control their fingers. Often I have observed bears looking in one direction and pointing their noses in a different direction while evaluating their surroundings. Eye contact in the bear world is a threat, so by gathering as much information as possible with their noses, bears can avoid making threats or aggressive postures.

While not making any noticeable threat postures, this black bear pauses to collect as much of my scent and pheromones as the air currents will provide him. Different animals use different primary sensory organs, and take in different information from the worlds that these primary organs dominate. Each different animal's intelligence is shaped through the filter of most-to-least-dominate sensory organs. Senses, ecology, morphology, perceptions, and circumstances also combine to uniquely shape an animal's understanding and overall theory of mind. Such different sensory inputs also combine with different physical outputs and yield different brains that process different types of information for different reasons. Any animal will therefore experience a different world than we do.

"Art is the child of Nature; yes, her darling child, in whom we trace the features of the mother's face, her aspect and her attitude."

—Henry Wadsworth Longfellow

This grizzly is displaying what I have come to term as the possum nose. I see this in wild grizzlies everywhere I find them.

Far left: This mother grizzly would place her face under water with her tongue extended. I was
curious enough about this behavior to investigate why she would do this.

"The secret of intuition— instant access to a massive memory, even if that memory is
olfaction sensory dominated. "There is no logical way to the discovery of these elemental laws.
There is only the way of intuition, which is helped by a feeling for the order lying behind the
appearance."

— Albert Einstein

"All I have seen teaches me to trust the Creator for all I have not seen."

— Ralph Waldo Emerson

"The wise man in the storm prays God, not for safety from danger, but for deliverance from fear. It is the storm within which endangers him, not the storm without."

— Ralph Waldo Emerson

"When a pine needle falls in the forest, the eagle sees it, the deer hears it, and the bear smells it."
— An old First Nation saying

Most bears are born with 42 teeth, which is usually ten more than people are born with. A bear's canines can extend from its gum line one and a half inches, while a human's extend less than a half inch.

All creatures have the ability to independently collect information (sensory system), act on that information (motor system), and store the results for future reference (memory), thus effectively making life possible.

Far left: At times, Casper's mother would leave her alone near river banks while she fished. Casper was keen to read the scent and pheromone markings left behind by other bears.

Center: There truly was no place Casper's mother could leave the young cub where other bears had not already been present, so it was important for Casper to know who else was in the neighborhood.

Right: Casper's mother would often plant her nose directly on a scent marked branch to gather messages left by other bears in the area. Although these scent markings are short lived story boards, they still give volumes of information about other bears in the surrounding area.

These places always seem like secrets that good friends quietly tell to their most treasured inner circles of friends.

"The teacher who is indeed wise does not bid you to enter the house of his wisdom but rather leads you to the threshold of your mind."

— Kahlil Gibran

After witnessing so much salmon roe flung into the air by feeding bears, I wondered if wild trout and bull char followed bears just to feast on their scraps.

This mother's work never seemed to be finished with three second-year cubs to feed and keep out of trouble.

"Mother is the name of God in the lips and hearts of little children."
— William Makepeace Thackerary

CHAPTER 7

Mother Grizzlies

DURING A TIME IN MY LIFE when free time was rare, I chose to go to Yellowstone in springtime as my ultimate destination for a renewing retreat. For one, Yellowstone was close to my home; my main reason to go to Yellowstone, however, was to see and photograph the numerous wildlife species found in the Yellowstone ecosystem, focusing mainly on wolves, bighorn rams, newborns, and most of all, the bears that migrate from their winter dens to the lush meadows along Yellowstone's numerous rivers and roadways. I observed that most roadside bears were either mothers with cubs or they were young adolescents. This was mainly because large male bears seek solitude, sequestering themselves away from people in their backcountry haunts. The roads of the heavily traveled tourist corridors offer a limited umbrella of protection from some of the predation of these larger beasts that roam the more remote areas.

My favorite Yellowstone bear to view and photograph was a grizzly known to most as 264, but whom I called

Obsidian, as I often located her near the Obsidian Cliff area. I captured many wonderful images of this bear with her cubs. When she felt calm and safe around a group of tourists, she would bring her cubs closer to show them off. Obsidian was a proud mother who enjoyed the company of people like no other wild grizzly I can recall. As this book focuses on photography since my cancer, I will reserve most images of Obsidian for future publications and have chosen here to showcase Casper and her mother.

Grizzly bears have one of the lowest reproductive rates of all terrestrial mammals. This is due in part to numerous ecological factors; for instance, if a sow does not have enough fat reserved for her winter den, she will abort her young. Also, grizzly bears do not reach sexual maturity until they are at least five years old. Mating season for most bear subsets usually occurs between early May to mid-July, with cubs born between the end of January and early March. Female grizzlies do not get pregnant immediately after mating. Following the procedure of delayed implantation, they can keep the fertilized egg floating in their womb until conditions are most favorable, generally during hibernation.

Only one in three grizzly bear sows breed in any given year, birthing one to four cubs, with the rare exception of a larger litter. Depending on their individual reproductive cycle, mothers wean their cubs after either two or three years. A grizzly sow may remain anestrous, or when she comes into estrus, fail to become fertilized and thus can fail to produce offspring for a span of four years or more. Predation of cubs by large boars or wolves can also greatly reduce a bear population.

Bear sows usually have four functional pectoral nipples and two functional inguinal nipples and usually six functional mammary glands. The mother grizzly pictured in this chapter is standing and exposing her four pectoral nipples. She is nursing the cubs that are fighting, which are also pictured. Her three cubs were always fighting, causing trouble, stealing food from each other, bawling, wandering off, and finding ways to be the most obnoxious bear cubs that I have ever seen. One night they chose to fight just below our lodgings, bawling, hissing, growling, clawing, and biting each other until daybreak. This made for some interesting conversation at breakfast. In spite of her cub's behavior, this mother grizzly was extremely tolerant and caring for her babes. Once in a while she would growl and give one a smack, but then she would calmly wade out into the river to catch them another salmon.

Casper and her mother reminded me of Obsidian (264) and her cubs. All bears have different personalities, just as people do, but Casper's mother and Obsidian seemed to be cut from the same mold. They both loved to show off their cubs. One difference though was that Obsidian was viewed by armies of tourists while Casper and her mother have been observed by less than two-dozen humans. One day while I was on the river photographing bears, Casper's mother brought her straw-colored child down to the upper riverbank, lay down, and nursed her. She could have easily wandered off into the woods to nurse, but she purposely chose our company. Bears nurse much the same as house cats do, purring included. Casper's mother purred so loudly that I thought she must have intended for us to hear it over the background sounds from the river. Maybe she used her purr intentionally to calm us down and promote a sense of peace in us and the surrounding area. Seeing bears like these is always a humbling privilege and I consider myself blessed to have enriched my soul with numerous such viewings and experiences.

*"Each of us is here for a brief sojourn; for what purpose he knows not, though he senses it.
But without deeper reflection one knows from daily life that one exists for other people."*

—Albert Einstein

These cubs are still nursing, can you believe it?

"What strange creatures brothers are!"
— Jane Austen

This cub went from fighting with its siblings to a relaxing
free float in the blink of an eye; no worries here.

"Sorrow looks back; Worry looks around; Faith looks up."
— Ralph Waldo Emerson

Casper giving me a classic "got milk" look. Her chin and nose were both covered with her mother's fresh milk.

"And this, our life, exempt from public haunt,
Finds tongues in trees, books in the running brooks,
Sermons in stones, and good in everything."
—William Shakespeare

"Treat the Earth well. It was not given to you by your parents, It was loaned to you by your children. We do not inherit the Earth from our ancestors, we borrow it from our children."

— Ancient Indian Proverb

"Two roads diverged in a yellow wood,
And sorry I could not travel both
And be one traveler, long I stood
And looked down one as far as I could

To where it bent in the undergrowth;
Then took the other, as just as fair,
And having perhaps the better claim,
Because it was grassy and wanted wear;

Though as for that the passing there
Had worn them really about the same,
And both that morning equally lay
In leaves no step had trodden black.

Oh, I kept the first for another day!
Yet knowing how way leads on to way,
I doubted if I should ever come back.
I shall be telling this with a sigh

Somewhere ages and ages hence:
Two roads diverged in a wood, and I—
I took the one less traveled by,
And that has made all the difference."

— Robert Frost

Right: What a splendid privilege it was to have breakfast with Casper and her mother as the first light brightened up the trees and lifted up the morning mist. Life is good.

"We'd never know how high we are, till we are called to rise; and then, if we are true to plan, our statures touch the sky"

— Emily Dickinson

Casper was actually licking leftover salmon roe from off her mother's chin. It did, though, look something like a kiss.

"The sunlight claps the earth, and the moonbeams kiss the sea:
what are all these kissings worth, if thou kiss not me?"
— Percy Bysshe Shelley

"Earth and sky, woods and fields, lakes and rivers, the mountain and the sea, are excellent schoolmasters, and teach some of us more than we can ever learn from books."

— Sir John Lubbock

The most overwhelming key to a cub's success is the spirited, confident, courageous and selfless involvement of their mother.

"Life is short and we never have enough time for gladdening the hearts of those who travel the way with us. Oh, be swift to love! Make haste to be kind."

— Henri Frederic Amiel

This splendid creature is grizzly #264 with one of her two cubs digging up worms of all things, and enjoying them with charming enthusiasm.

"All my life through, the new sights of Nature made me rejoice like a child."
— Marie Curie

The following has been adapted and condensed from The Alaskan Daily News:
"Abandoned by his mother and seemingly left for dead, a yearling grizzly bear cub at Katmai National Park and Preserve has been adopted by another female bear." Holly, formally recognized as brown bear 435, is a Katmai brown bear between 18 and 20 years old. Holly apparently has an aptitude for raising young bears as she was previously known to have nursed one of her own yearling cubs with a broken leg back to health. This year Holly outdid herself and adopted an abandoned cub while still nursing an adolescent of her own. The rescued cub was abandoned by his mother and apparently left for dead while she ran off with a male bear to mate. Nowadays, rangers at Brooks Falls describe Holly as a supermom:
"We don't know what caused Holly to adopt him. It may just be a powerful maternal instinct," said Roy Wood Katmai's chief of interpretation. *"Anytime the sow has cubs, it is a strain on her system, and having to feed them, nurse them or share food with them could drag her health down, and it's possible they won't make it through the winter,"* Roy Wood added.

Left: I originally thought that the adopted cub was the smaller of the two; as it turned out, it was the larger cub—seen here chasing the biological cub up a tree as Holly calmly fished.

Right: Holly in all her splendid glory amidst nature's golden crown.

"Had I not seen the Sun,
I could have borne the shade,
But Light a newer Wilderness,
My Wilderness has made."
— Emily Dickinson

*"Everything you look at can become a fairy tale
and you can get a story from everything you touch."*

— Hans Christian Andersen

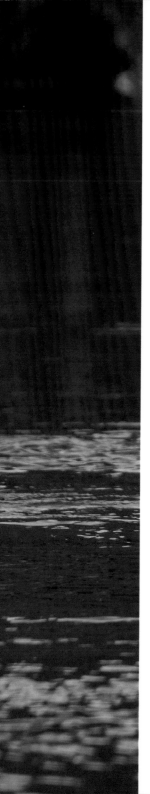

"Listen to the wind, it talks.
Listen to the silence, it speaks.
Listen to your heart, it knows."-
— Native American Proverb

CHAPTER 8

Reflections

MY REFLECTIONS began in the infusion room. I was diagnosed with B-cell lymphoma on December 16, 2008, after biopsy results from two masses growing in my lymphatic system tested positive. I was devastated. Cancer was something that happened to other people, not me. After a bone-marrow biopsy, PET scan, and other tests, I began chemotherapy with R-CHOP on January 8, 2009.

I was new to all of this, and I was learning things about cancer that I never wanted to know. B-cell lymphoma was killing folks a decade earlier, before my diagnosis. Five years before I was diagnosed, people with this type of lymphoma were in and out of remission for several years until they usually died from the disease. I am living proof of the importance of cancer research and am grateful to the army of medical pioneers who have devoted their lives to save mine and yours or the life of someone you love.

During infusion, you have many hours to reflect. Reflection is an escape from the business of infusion. My infusions lasted nine hours, so I had a few more hours of

quiet contemplation than most patients. Every detail of life becomes dead serious in infusion rooms, and thoughts tend to drift toward things that are most important to you. I mostly thought about my family, encountering so many unresolved issues and haunting memories. Infusion is where you make promises to yourself—the kind you intend to keep. Most of my promises involved my family, but at times I wondered if I would ever again be outdoors with a camera in hand.

When I saw other photographers' images from the Chilcotin Mountains grizzly-bear tour, the first thing that I focused on were the wonderful reflections. In my past, I photographed many bears in Yellowstone and Glacier National Parks. I often saw bears close to rivers and lakes, but rare were the opportunities to capture bears with their reflections. But here on this river, deep in the Chilcotin Range, it seemed that every picture had a reflection, so I booked the tour.

On day one, from the small boat dock I saw many

reflections on the river, all with different colors and lighting. My thoughts raced straight back to the promises I made to myself and the things that I sincerely hoped to do after I recovered from cancer. I was now living those dreams. I felt a surreal, déjà vu utopia as energy charged through my post-cancer body, back from the dead and living out my dreams. In the following days, I photographed so many grizzlies with their reflections that I lost count. Every bend in the river came with its own lighting and colors ranging from greens to browns, yellows to vivid fall bursts. The river looked like a kaleidoscope as hues changed by the minute and shadows grew, darkened, and then disappeared before our eyes. There must be places like this in heaven, because this riparian river system is a preview of heaven on earth.

"Come forth into the light of things. Let nature be your teacher."
— William Wordsworth

"The tints of autumn...a mighty flower garden
blossoming under the spell of the enchanter, frost."
— John Greenleaf Whittier

"A painter should begin every canvas with a wash of black, because all things in nature are dark except where exposed by the light."

— Leonardo da Vinci

Drink it in.

"We never know the worth of water till the well is dry."
— Thomas Fuller

*"What lies behind us and what lies before us
are tiny matters compared to what lies within us."*
— Ralph Waldo Emerson

"Guard well your spare moments. They are like uncut diamonds. Discard them and their value will never be known. Improve them and they will become the brightest gems in a useful life."

—Ralph Waldo Emerson

"No spring nor summer beauty hath such grace as I have seen in one autumnal face."
— John Donne

"*Time is*
Too Slow for those who Wait,   *Too Short for those who Rejoice;*
Too Swift for those who Fear,   *But for those who Love,*
Too Long for those who Grieve,   *Time is not.*"
— Henry van Dyke

"How strange that nature does not knock, and yet does not intrude!"
— Emily Dickinson

"Those who dream by day are cognizant of many things which escape those who dream only by night. In their gray visions they obtain glimpses of eternity, and thrill, in waking, to find that they have been upon the verge of the great secret. In snatches, they learn something of the wisdom which is of good, and more of the mere knowledge which is of evil."

— Edgar Allan Poe

"Humankind has not woven the web of life. We are but one thread within it. Whatever we do to the web, we do to ourselves. All things are bound together. All things connect."

— Chief Seattle

"Dwell as near as possible to the channel in which your life flows."
— Henry David Thoreau

*"No man ever steps in the same river twice, for it is never the same river —
and he's not the same man."*
— Heraclitus

"There never was a moment in my life, when I felt so in the Presence, as I do now. I feel as if the Almighty were so real, and so near, that I could reach out and touch Him, as I could this wonderful work of His, if I dared. I feel like saying to Him: 'To the extent of my brain power I realize Your presence, and all it is in me to comprehend of Your power. Help me to learn, even this late, the lessons of Your wonderful creations. Help me to unshackle and expand my soul to the fullest realization of Your wonders. Almighty God, make me bigger, make me broader!'"

— Gene Stratton-Porter, *A Girl of the Limberlost*

"The central thing for which Conservation stands is to make this country the best possible place to live in, both for us and for our descendants."

— Gifford Pinchot

*"Observe the Wonders as they occur around You.
Don't claim them.
Feel the artistry moving through and Be Silent."*
— Rumi

"An old man going a lone highway,   The old man crossed in the twilight dim;
Came at the evening, cold and gray,   The sullen stream had no fear for him;
To a chasm, vast, and deep and wide,   But he turned, when safe on the other side,
Through which was flowing a sullen tide.   And built a bridge to span the tide."

— Will Allen Dromgoole

"Old times never come back and I suppose it's just as well.
What comes back is a new morning every day in the year, and that's better.
— George E. Woodberry

"If God did not exist, He would have to be invented. But all nature cries aloud that he does exist: that there is a supreme intelligence, an immense power, an admirable order, and everything teaches us our own dependence on it."

— Voltaire

"God writes the gospel not in the Bible alone,
but on trees and flowers and clouds and stars."
— Unknown, however commonly attributed to Martin Luther

Praise ye the Lord. Praise God in His sanctuary: praise Him in the firmament of His power.
Praise Him for His mighty acts: praise Him according to His excellent greatness.
— *Psalms 150: 1-2*

Left: *"Greatness is not in where we stand, but in what direction we are moving. We must sail sometimes with the wind and sometimes against it — but sail we must, and not drift, nor lie at anchor."*

— Oliver Wendell Holmes, Jr.

The Ocean Light II and her crew have been offering exciting trips of exploration on the British Columbia coast for more than 30 years. With the Ocean Light II as a base, tours to the Great Bear Rain Forest, Spirit Bear Viewing and other explorations of the wilderness coasts found along the Inside Passage of scenic British Columbia become experiences of a lifetime.

Ocean Light II
Email : adventure@oceanlight2.bc.ca
Phone: 1.604.328.5339
www.oceanlight2.bc.ca

Left: *"The time of the falling leaves has come again. Once more in our morning walk we tread upon carpets of gold and crimson, of brown and bronze, woven by the winds or the rains out of these delicate textures while we slept."*
— John Burroughs

The McLean's Tsylos Park Lodge has been in operation since 1957 and is a perfect dream vacation destination featuring river fly fishing trips, wilderness horse pack trips, and some of the best grizzly bear viewing trips found anywhere on this planet. Each of these tours are accompanied with exceptional guides and service.

Tsylos Park Lodge & Adventures
Williams Lake, British Columbia, Canada V2G 4P2
Email: tsylos@tsylos.com
Phone: 1.800.487.9567
www.tsylos.com

"The world is round, so travellers tell,
And straight through reach the track,
Trudge on, trudge on, 'twill all be well,
The way will guide one back."

— A.E. Housman